Patrick Learns About Parkinson's Disease

A Story of a Special Bond Between Friends

by Kim Gosselin

Written for the Special Family and Friends™ series

JayJo Books, L.L.C.
Publishing Special Books for Special Kids®

Patrick Learns About Parkinson's Disease

© 2002 Kim Gosselin

Edited by Karen Schader

Published by

JayJo Books

A Guidance Channel Company

Publishing Special Books for Special Kids®

JayJo Books is a publisher of books to help teachers, parents, and children cope with chronic illnesses, special needs, and health education in classroom, family, and social settings.

Library of Congress Control Number 2001097488

ISBN 1-891383-18-3

Second book in our *Special Family and Friends*™ series

For information about
Premium and Special Sales, contact:

JayJo Books Special Sales Office

P.O. Box 213

Valley Park, MO 63088-0213

636-861-1331

jayjobooks@aol.com

www.jayjo.com

For all other information, contact:

JayJo Books

135 Dupont Street, P.O. Box 760

Plainview, NY 11803-0760

1-800-999-6884

jayjobooks@guidancechannel.com

www.jayjo.com

Dedication

Dedicated to all those who live life to the fullest, in spite of Parkinson's disease. May you have long and happy lives.

About the Author

Recognizing the need for books to help children understand adult medical conditions, Kim Gosselin created the Special Family and Friends™ series. She is the author of the first book in the series, Allie Learns About Alzheimer's Disease, which draws on her own experience when her grandmother was diagnosed with Alzheimer's disease.

Kim is the author of 12 children's health education books. She began her writing career with a heartfelt desire and determination to educate the classmates of children with special needs and/or chronic conditions. Kim created the Special Kids in School® series, which covers topics such as diabetes, asthma, allergies, seizure disorders, attention deficit disorder, cerebral palsy, cancer, and cystic fibrosis. She also created the Substance Free Kids® series and the Healthy Habits for Kids® series.

Kim now resides and writes in Missouri. She is extremely committed to bringing the young reader quality health education, while raising important funds for medical research. She is an avid supporter of the American Lung Association, American Cancer Society, the Epilepsy Foundation of America, American Diabetes Association, Juvenile Diabetes Research Foundation, and CHADD. For her work with children with chronic diseases, Kim received the National American Lung Association Presidential Award. Kim is also a member of the Authors Guild, the Publishers Marketing Association, and the Society of Children's Book Writers and Illustrators.

"Hi, Mr. Jennings," Patrick called, waving to his next-door neighbor. Mr. Jennings smiled and waved back. Patrick saw him stoop to pick up his newspaper, nearly falling as he tried to stand up. Grabbing onto the mailbox, Mr. Jennings regained his balance. Patrick kept a watchful eye on Mr. Jennings as he shuffled toward his back door. He was worried about his friend.

Mr. Jennings hadn't been acting quite right during the last several months. Patrick had seen his hand shake, sometimes for no reason at all. Mr. Jennings' words sounded different than they used to. It seemed like he was beginning to talk softer or slower, somehow.

Even Patrick's mother had noticed Mr. Jennings losing his balance once in a while. In fact, she was so concerned that she scheduled a vacation day at work just to take him to the doctor. Mr. Jennings needed a good checkup!

Patrick didn't want to think about doctors now, though. Tonight he was going to the circus with Mr. Jennings! Patrick's heart quickened as he thought of the two circus tickets his mother was holding for safekeeping in the kitchen.

Mr. Jennings had always been an important part of Patrick's life. Soon after Patrick was born, his mother suddenly became a single parent.
With no other family, Mr. Jennings was like a grandfather to Patrick. They did almost everything together.

After school, Mr. Jennings often helped Patrick with his homework. On weekends, Mr. Jennings came along with Patrick's mother to watch him play baseball. Sometimes, the two of them rode the city bus to the big movie theatre with the soft velvet seats.

Sunday afternoons were the most fun, though. Patrick got to help Mr. Jennings with his woodworking projects. Lions, bears, dogs, horses, cats, and tigers sat neatly displayed on shelves in Mr. Jennings' old backyard shed. Mr. Jennings had carefully carved each and every one of them from a single block of wood.

Finally, it was almost time to go to the circus! On Patrick's bed lay his very best pair of jeans and pullover sweater. Patrick got dressed, combed his hair, and raced into the living room where his mother sat reading a book. "How handsome you look," she said, smiling up at him. Patrick blushed, grinning from ear to ear.

Next door, Mr. Jennings adjusted his red bow tie. Glancing into the bathroom mirror, he saw his hand trembling again. Although Mr. Jennings felt a little scared, he wasn't going to let anything spoil his special circus outing with Patrick. "Besides, I'll be getting a checkup tomorrow," he thought to himself.

Patrick's mother kissed her son goodbye and gave Mr. Jennings a great big hug. Soon the two were out the door and off to the bus stop down the street. Patrick's mother worried, noticing that Mr. Jennings took shorter steps than usual. He seemed to be holding on to Patrick's hand for support. She would be glad when Mr. Jennings had his checkup!

The "Big Top" was a spectacular sight! Brightly colored balloons in red, orange, green, yellow, and blue floated near the striped ceiling of the enormous tent. Pretty girls in spangled blue satin costumes rode graceful white horses with purple feather plumes. Clowns, dressed in polka dots, tumbled nearby. The smell of hot dogs, roasted peanuts, buttery popcorn, and sweet cotton candy filled the air.

Mr. Jennings' tickets were the best in the house, front row and center! Mr. Jennings and Patrick sat down in their lucky seats. Happily, they settled in for the time of their lives!

Music blared aloud while a juggler in the right circus ring tossed red rubber balls up into the air. The juggler accidentally dropped a ball. Quickly, a clown with bright green hair scooped it up and tossed it back. The crowd roared! The clown kept doing funny tricks to distract the juggler even more.

High, high overhead, a young man in a leotard costume carefully walked the tightrope above the left circus ring. Suddenly, the crowd screamed! The tightrope walker lost his balance and fell down, down, down to the safety net below. Then he bounced to his feet with a smile on his face. The crowd cheered!

The magical night ended all too soon for both Mr. Jennings and Patrick. Taking the last bus home, a drowsy Patrick fell fast asleep leaning on the older man's shoulder. It wasn't long before Mr. Jennings dropped him safely into the arms of his waiting mother. She tucked Patrick into bed. A sleepy smile spread across his face.

Mr. Jennings said good night and headed next door. He was tired too! As he crawled into bed, his legs felt so tight he could barely move them. His leg muscles felt sore. Even so, nothing could spoil the evening he had just spent with Patrick. Mr. Jennings quickly drifted off to sleep. Visions of cotton candy, circus clowns, and the sounds of Patrick's giggle filled his pleasant dreams.

The next day Mr. Jennings went for his checkup. The doctors checked Mr. Jennings' heart and his blood pressure. They asked him lots of questions too. Mr. Jennings had blood tests done, and a special x-ray test called an MRI. Mr. Jennings was glad Patrick's mother came along for support, since they were like family to each other.

After a long morning of tests, Mr. Jennings and Patrick's mother were asked to meet with a special doctor called a neurologist. The doctor was a very nice woman, who spoke gently to them, explaining what Mr. Jennings' test results meant.

Mr. Jennings' neurologist thought he had a condition called Parkinson's disease. She told them that some of the nerve cells in Mr. Jennings' brain didn't make enough of a special chemical it needed called dopamine. Because of this, Mr. Jennings was having problems moving and speaking clearly.

Suddenly Mr. Jennings understood why his hand had been trembling. Now he knew why he sometimes had trouble moving his legs or lost his balance. No wonder his muscles felt stiff and his speech sounded different than it used to. Without enough dopamine, his brain couldn't send the right messages to his body. Now it all made sense to him!

Nobody really knew what caused Parkinson's disease. Not even Mr. Jennings' neurologist! Getting Parkinson's disease wasn't anyone's fault. It just happened and it wasn't contagious. Nobody could ever catch Parkinson's disease from Mr. Jennings or anyone else!

The neurologist explained that there were five different stages of Parkinson's disease. Everyone's condition was different. Hopefully, Mr. Jennings would live a long, long time without feeling any worse. Best of all, there were many different kinds of medicines that might help him feel much better!

The doctor gave Patrick's mother some prescriptions and her phone number to call if either of them had any more questions. She handed them several pamphlets about Parkinson's disease. They learned the importance of exercising properly, eating the right foods, and getting lots of rest. Afterwards, the two of them rode the elevator to the first floor, where Mr. Jennings signed up for his first support group meeting. There, he would meet lots of other people living with Parkinson's disease. It made him feel better to know that he was not the only one.

The drive home was very quiet. Suddenly, Mr. Jennings felt sad. So did Patrick's mother. That was a normal feeling, the doctor had told them earlier. They both knew that Mr. Jennings' life was changing. How he wished everything could be the way it was long ago. Would Patrick still want to be his special friend?

Patrick's mother reassured Mr. Jennings that Patrick would always love him, no matter what! Besides, Mr. Jennings had been helping Patrick and his mother for many years. Now, it was their turn. After all, he was just like family to them! Patrick's mother invited Mr. Jennings over for dinner that evening. She didn't want him to eat alone after such a long day.

Patrick's mother dropped Mr. Jennings off at his neat stucco house so he could get some rest before dinnertime. She parked her car next door, and decided to talk to Patrick. He was just getting home from school. She carefully explained to him all about their visit to Mr. Jennings' doctors. Patrick seemed to understand. Best of all, he understood that Parkinson's disease was only a very small part of Mr. Jennings. No matter what, they would always be friends!

After dinner that night, Patrick's mother began to clear the kitchen table. The older man and the younger boy went outside to sit on the porch swing. "Remember the tightrope walker we saw at the circus?" asked Mr. Jennings. "Sure I do," Patrick replied. "It was scary when he fell down off the rope." "That's kind of how I feel," said Mr. Jennings. "I'm a little scared. I know I'll lose my balance sometimes too." "But just like the circus man," Patrick interrupted, "you'll have a safety net ... me and my mom! You'll see, you'll bounce back smiling too!"

Patrick snuggled up to the older man. Right at that moment, Mr. Jennings couldn't have felt happier. Suddenly, he wasn't so afraid anymore. Like Patrick's mother had said, Patrick would always love him, no matter what.

"And, just like the juggler in the circus," Mr. Jennings whispered into Patrick's ear, "I might drop the ball once in a while, but you can always toss it back to me!"

THE END

To order additional copies of Patrick Learns About Parkinson's Disease or inquire about our quantity discounts for schools, hospitals, and affiliated organizations, contact us at 1-800-999-6884.

From our *Special Kids in School*® series

Taking A.D.D. to School
Taking Asthma to School
Taking Autism to School
Taking Cancer to School
Taking Cerebral Palsy to School
Taking Cystic Fibrosis to School
Taking Diabetes to School
Taking Down Syndrome to School
Taking Dyslexia to School
Taking Food Allergies to School
Taking Seizure Disorders to School
Taking Tourette Syndrome to School
...and others coming soon!

From our *Healthy Habits for Kids*® series

There's a Louse in My House
A Fun Story about Kids and Head Lice

From our *Special Family and Friends*™ series

Allie Learns About Alzheimer's Disease
A Family Story about Love, Patience, and Acceptance

And from our *Substance Free Kids*® series

Smoking STINKS!!™
A Heartwarming Story about the Importance of Avoiding Tobacco

Other books available now!

SPORTSercise!
A School Story about
Exercise-Induced Asthma

ZooAllergy
A Fun Story about Allergy
and Asthma Triggers

Rufus Comes Home
Rufus the Bear with Diabetes™
A Story about Diagnosis and
Acceptance

The ABC's of Asthma
An Asthma Alphabet Book
for Kids of All Ages

Taming the Diabetes Dragon
A Story about Living Better
with Diabetes

Trick-or-Treat for Diabetes
A Halloween Story for Kids
Living with Diabetes

A portion of the proceeds from all our publications is donated to various charities to help fund important medical research and education. We work hard to make a difference in the lives of children with chronic conditions and/or special needs. Thank you for your support.